for William Howard

24 Preludes and Fugues

T0057042

HOWARD SKEMPTON

1

Allegro

mp

Adagio
(non stacc.)

p

24 Preludes and Fugues were composed for William Howard who gave the first performance on 27 May 2019 at the Hay Festival, followed by the London premiere on 12 February 2020 at Kings Place. A recording of this work is available on the album *Howard Skempton: Piano Works*, released by Orchid Classics in 2020.

Duration: 22 mins

© Oxford University Press 2020

Printed in Great Britain

OXFORD UNIVERSITY PRESS, MUSIC DEPARTMENT, GREAT CLARENDON STREET, OXFORD OX2 6DP

The Moral Rights of the Composer have been asserted. Photocopying this copyright material is ILLEGAL.

2
Moderato
mp
Larghetto
mp

3
Allegro
mf
Andante
mp

4

Moderato
mp
1.
2.
Adagio
p

6
Vivo
mf
Fine
D.S. al Fine
Adagio
2·3·2
mp

7

8

9

Moderato

p

Adagio

mf

10
Allegro
mp
Moderato
p

11
Andante
mp

12

13

14

15

16

17

18

19

20

21

22

23

24

Music originated by Julian Elloway
Printed in England by Halstan & Co. Ltd, Amersham, Bucks.